The Art of Good Food

POTATO
FILLINGS

The Art of Good Food

POTATO FILLINGS

JON HIGGINS

Illustrated by

PAUL COLLICUTT

CHARTWELL BOOKS, INC.

The Art of Good Food

Potato Fillings

Designed and created by

THE BRIDGEWATER BOOK COMPANY LTD

Designer Sarah Stanley

Editor Donna Wood

Managing Editor Anna Clarkson

Illustrations Paul Collicutt

Page make-up Martyn Feather

CHARTWELL BOOKS

A division of Book Sales, Inc.

POST OFFICE BOX 7100

114 Northfield Avenue

Edison, N.J. 08837

CLB 4588

© 1996 COLOUR LIBRARY BOOKS LTD

Godalming, Surrey, U.K.

All rights reserved.

Color separation by Sussex Repro, England

Printed and bound in Singapore by Tien Wah Press

ISBN 0-7858-0376-9

Contents

Introduction

The humble potato is part of everyone's diet; in one form or another we eat this most versatile of vegetables at least once a day. We boil, mash and fry away week in, week out, without actually thinking about its other possibilities. Yet what could be simpler than scrubbing the skins and placing the potatoes in a preheated oven for an hour or so, or if you lead a hectic lifestyle, microwaving for a mere ten minutes?

Of course, cooking the potato is only the beginning. There is an almost endless variety of fillings that can be used to bring excitement to mealtimes, from the rich and exotic sauces ideal for candlelit suppers, to the quick and healthy fillings for those on the move, but who need to watch their waistlines.

The collection of recipes contained in this book has been chosen to appeal to the widest range of tastes, from young to old, palates that vary from the straightforward to the sophisticated and from quickly prepared dishes to those that are a little more involved. There is also a section especially for vegetarians.

CHOOSING POTATOES FOR BAKING

Choose potatoes of roughly similar size, approximately 8–10 ounces in weight is ideal. Because potatoes are a product of Mother Nature they do not grow to identical shapes and sizes, so pick carefully and avoid any that are scuffed or green, or have deep eyes which can make cleaning difficult. Also avoid any potatoes that have excess soil adhering to them; this is tedious to remove and since potatoes are usually sold by weight you will end up paying for soil! Almost all varieties of old potatoes (also known as maincrop potatoes) are suitable for baking, but Maris Piper, King Edward, Desirée and Cara are particularly good. At one time it would have been impossible to tell one type from another unless you had extensive knowledge of potatoes, but now that most retailers clearly show variety names at sales points, you can now purchase the type you want.

STORING POTATOES

If necessary, remove the potatoes from their polyethylene packaging and store them unwashed in a dark, cool place that gets plenty of air. This will ensure that the potatoes stay in the peak of condition.

TO BAKE A POTATO IN A CONVENTIONAL OVEN

1   Preheat the oven to 425°F.

2   Scrub the potatoes well under cold running water. Prick the skins all over with a fork to allow steam to escape during cooking and prevent the skins from bursting open. If desired, brush the skins with a little oil; this will give a glossy appearance to the surface of the potato when it is baked.

3   Put the potatoes directly on the oven shelf and leave to cook for 1–1¼ hours or until the potato feels soft when lightly squeezed. You can reduce cooking time a little by spearing the potatoes onto metal skewers.

TO BAKE A POTATO IN A MICROWAVE OVEN

1   Scrub the potatoes well under cold running water and prick the skins with a fork to prevent bursting.

2   Place the potatoes well apart in the microwave oven on a few sheets of paper towel, and cook on full power. Allow one potato about 8 minutes cooking time, two potatoes about 15 minutes and four potatoes about 25 minutes.

Using a microwave oven is fine to bake potatoes if you are in a hurry, but they will never equal the delicious combination of crunchy skin and fluffy insides obtained by conventional cooking methods.

Spice-dusted Beef with Coconut Sauce

SERVES 4

This exotic mix of flavors adds a touch of mystery to mealtimes

INGREDIENTS
4 large baking potatoes
1 pound sirloin steak
2 teaspoons garam masala
½ teaspoon turmeric
vegetable oil
1 onion, finely chopped
½ ounce fresh ginger, finely grated
2 ounces fresh grated coconut
⅔ cup heavy cream
salt and pepper

Begin by setting the potatoes to bake in a hot oven as recommended in the introduction.

Using a sharp knife slice the steak into thin strips and lay them out on a plate. Mix together the garam masala and turmeric and sprinkle the mixture evenly over the strips of steak, turning to ensure that they are well coated.

Heat 2 tablespoons of vegetable oil in a frying pan until smoking then add the steak a few strips at a time and quickly fry on both sides until they are nicely browned.

Remove the meat from the pan and place on some paper towel to soak up any excess oil.

When all the meat has been cooked, add a further tablespoon of oil to the pan and fry the chopped onion until nicely browned, add the fresh ginger and coconut to the pan and stir for a few minutes.

Lower the heat and add the heavy cream, stirring for a few minutes until all the flavors have combined and the sauce is hot.

Return the spicy beef to the pan and coat well in the sauce. Test a little on a teaspoon and correct the seasoning.

Cut the baked potatoes two-thirds of the way through and gently ease them open, fluff up the insides with a fork. Divide the topping among the potatoes and serve.

TIME: *Preparation takes about 10 minutes.*
Cooking takes approximately 15 minutes.

12

Creamy Bacon & Mushrooms

SERVES 4

Use plain or smoked bacon according to taste

INGREDIENTS

4 large baking potatoes
6 slices smoked back bacon
¼ cup butter
2 cloves garlic, crushed
6 scallions, sliced
8 ounces mushrooms, sliced
1 teaspoon cornstarch
a little milk
pinch of grated nutmeg
7-ounce carton full-fat fromage frais
salt and pepper

▌Begin by setting the potatoes to bake in a hot oven as recommended in the introduction.
▌Remove the rind from the bacon and discard. Cut the bacon into strips.
▌Melt the butter in a frying pan and sauté the bacon and garlic until the bacon begins to brown. Stir in the scallions and mushrooms and sauté for 5–6 minutes or until the mushrooms are soft.

▌Mix the cornstarch to a smooth paste with a little milk, then stir into the pan. Add the nutmeg, then stir in the fromage frais. Bring carefully to simmering point and simmer for 2 minutes; do not to let the mixture boil. Season to taste with salt, pepper and nutmeg.
▌When the potatoes are cooked, cut a cross in the top of each one. Gently squeeze each potato to open out the cross slightly.
▌Spoon the mushroom mixture on top and serve immediately.

TIME: *Preparation takes about 15 minutes. Cooking takes approximately 10 minutes.*
WATCHPOINT: *Do not use the very low-fat fromage frais in this recipe because it will curdle.*

14

Honey-glazed Chicken Bites

SERVES 4

This is a very simple but delicious topping

INGREDIENTS

4 large baking potatoes

12 ounces cooked warm chicken,
skinned and cut into chunks

1 bunch of scallions, roughly chopped

¼ cup walnuts, roughly chopped

⅓ cup clear honey

½ teaspoon cayenne pepper

salt and pepper

Begin by setting the potatoes to bake in a hot oven as recommended in the introduction.

In a large mixing bowl combine all the remaining ingredients and carefully mix together.

When cooked, cut a deep cross almost through the potatoes and allow them to fan out. Melt a little butter into each potato and spoon on the topping.

TIME: *Preparation takes about 10 minutes.*

SERVING IDEA: *This is delicious for lunch on a hot summer's day if served with a fresh green salad and a glass of chilled white wine.*

Spicy Tomato & Chorizo Sausage

SERVES 4

A *Mediterranean combination of spicy sausage and fresh tomatoes*

INGREDIENTS

4 large baking potatoes

2 tablespoons olive oil

1 Spanish onion, chopped

3 cloves garlic, crushed

1 teaspoon paprika

1 pound tomatoes, preferably plum,
skinned and roughly chopped

5 ounces chorizo or other spicy sausage, sliced

Begin by setting the potatoes to bake in a hot oven as recommended in the introduction.

Heat the oil in a saucepan and fry the onion until soft and beginning to brown.

Add the garlic and paprika and fry for a further 2 minutes.

Stir in the chopped tomatoes and bring gently to a boil.

Add the chorizo to the pan. Reduce the heat and simmer gently for 20–25 minutes.

When the potatoes are cooked, cut a cross in the top of each one. Gently squeeze each potato to open out the cross slightly.

Pile the sausage mixture on top and serve.

TIME: *Preparation takes about 10 minutes. Cooking takes approximately 30 minutes.*

17

Ham & Broccoli Stuffed Potatoes

SERVES 4

A *great supper dish for all the family*

INGREDIENTS

4 large baking potatoes
8 ounces broccoli flowerets
salt and pepper
2 tablespoons butter
2 tablespoons all-purpose flour
1¼ cups milk
pinch of grated nutmeg
2 ounces corn
6 ounces ham, diced

▮ Begin by setting the potatoes to bake in a hot oven as recommended in the introduction.
▮ Blanch the broccoli in lightly salted boiling water for 5 minutes and drain well.
▮ Melt the butter in a saucepan. Stir in the flour and cook over a low heat for 1 minute.

▮ Gradually add the milk a little at a time until it has all been incorporated and you have a beautifully smooth sauce of coating consistency.
▮ Season to taste with salt, pepper and nutmeg.
▮ Add the blanched broccoli, the corn and ham, and heat through.
▮ When the potatoes are cooked, cut in half and scoop out the flesh. Mash well.
▮ Add the broccoli and ham mixture and mix gently until well combined.
▮ Spoon back into the potato skins and serve.

TIME: *Preparation takes about 5 minutes. Cooking takes approximately 10 minutes.*
WATCHPOINT: *Be careful not to overcook the broccoli at the beginning or it will disintegrate completely.*

18

Savory Pork

SERVES 4

The perfect accompaniment for baked potatoes

INGREDIENTS

4 large baking potatoes

2 tablespoons sunflower oil

1 large onion, chopped

2 cloves garlic, crushed

12 ounces lean ground pork

1 green bell pepper, seeded and chopped

4 ounces mushrooms, sliced

14-ounce can chopped tomatoes with herbs

2 tablespoons tomato paste

¼ cup butter

⅔ cup heavy cream

chopped parsley to garnish

▌ Begin by setting the potatoes to bake in a hot oven as recommended in the introduction. Heat the oil in a frying pan and fry the onion until just soft. Add the garlic and fry for 1 minute. Add the pork and fry until brown.

▌ Stir in the pepper, mushrooms, tomatoes and paste, bring to a boil, then simmer for 30 minutes.

▌ When the potatoes are cooked, cut a wedge out of each one. Scoop out the flesh and mash with the butter and cream until smooth. Fill each potato skin half full with the mash and spoon in hot ground pork until it just overflows. Sprinkle with parsley and serve.

TIME: *Preparation takes about 10 minutes. Cooking takes approximately 40 minutes.*

Easy Chili

SERVES 4

This filling is simple to prepare

INGREDIENTS

4 large baking potatoes

1 tablespoon sunflower oil

1 small onion, chopped

12 ounces lean ground beef

1 teaspoon chili powder

⅔ cup beef stock

7-ounce can red kidney beans, drained and rinsed

14-ounce can chopped tomatoes

1 tablespoon tomato paste

▌ Begin by setting the potatoes to bake in a hot oven as recommended in the introduction.

▌ Heat the oil in a saucepan and fry the onion until soft. Add the meat and cook until browned.

▌ Stir in the chili powder and cook for 1 minute.

▌ Stir the stock, beans, tomatoes and tomato paste into the pan and bring gently to a boil.

▌ Reduce the heat and simmer for 20 minutes or until the meat is tender.

▌ When the potatoes are cooked, cut the tops off, mash the flesh and pour the chili over the top.

TIME: *Preparation takes about 5 minutes. Cooking takes approximately 35 minutes.*

19

Sausage, Egg & Bacon

SERVES 4

This traditional and popular combination is an unusual way of serving potatoes

INGREDIENTS
4 large baking potatoes
6 thin pork sausages
6 slices bacon
2 tablespoons butter
4 teaspoon brown fruity sauce
2 hard-boiled eggs, roughly chopped

❚ Begin by setting the potatoes to bake in a hot oven as recommended in the introduction.

❚ Cut the sausages in half to form smaller sausages.

❚ Remove the rind from the bacon and discard. Stretch the bacon with the back of a knife and cut each slice into two pieces.

❚ Wrap each sausage in a piece of bacon and thread 3 sausages on 1 cocktail stick, to make 4 mini kebabs.

❚ Place on a baking sheet and cook along with the potatoes for 25 minutes, or cook under a preheated broiler.

❚ Cut the tops off the cooked potatoes and scoop the flesh into a bowl. Mash well with the butter and fruity sauce.

❚ Stir in the chopped egg. Spoon the mixture back into the potato skins and return to the oven for 10 minutes.

❚ Top the potatoes with the sausage kebabs and serve with baked beans.

TIME: *Preparation takes about 10 minutes. Cooking takes approximately 10 minutes, plus reheating.*

MICROWAVE NOTES: *If cooking the potatoes in a microwave, reheat for 2–3 minutes on 100% (high).*

20

Broiled Chicken with Garlic Butter

SERVES 4

For a more subtle flavor you can use less garlic if you wish

INGREDIENTS
4 large baking potatoes
¼ cup unsalted butter
4 cloves garlic
salt and pepper
4 skinned chicken breasts
½ cup thick Greek yogurt

Begin by setting the potatoes to bake in a hot oven as recommended in the introduction.

Remove the butter from the refrigerator and allow it to come to room temperature.

Peel the garlic, place on a nonabsorbent surface and roughly chop. Sprinkle with a little salt and, using the side of a knife, crush the garlic under the blade and slowly work it into a paste.

Place the garlic paste in a mixing bowl with the butter and beat well until they are thoroughly combined.

Lay the chicken breasts on a tinfoil-covered baking sheet and season well with salt and freshly ground black pepper. Smear two-thirds of the garlic butter all over the meat.

When the potatoes are three-quarters cooked, place the prepared chicken under a preheated broiler and cook for 10 minutes on each side or until browned.

Make a deep cut into each baked potato and rub some of the remaining garlic butter over the surface of the flesh, then place a piece of broiled chicken into each potato and top with a spoonful of Greek yogurt.

Finish with a twist of fresh black pepper and serve immediately.

TIME: *Preparation takes about 15 minutes. Cooking takes approximately 20 minutes.*

22

Chinese Beef & Green Pepper

SERVES 4

A *popular Chinese dish that lends itself very well to baked potatoes*

INGREDIENTS

4 large baking potatoes
1 pound fillet steak
2 tablespoons sherry
2 tablespoons soya sauce
1 tablespoon cornstarch
3 tablespoons oil
2 seeded and chopped green bell peppers
2 tablespoons oyster sauce
meat stock

Begin by setting the potatoes to bake in a hot oven as recommended in the introduction.

Cut the beef into 2-inch slices across the grain and place in a mixing bowl. Combine the sherry, soya sauce and cornstarch and pour over the sliced beef, mix well to ensure it is fully combined and put aside to marinate.

When the potatoes are cooked, remove the beef from the marinade and drain off any excess liquid. Heat 2 tablespoons of oil in a wok and quickly stir-fry the beef for about 1 minute or until just cooked, remove from the wok and set aside.

Heat the remaining oil and add the chopped pepper to the pan. Stir-fry until the pepper begins to soften; then return the beef to the pan along with the oyster sauce and sufficient stock to make a small amount of gravy.

Toss together briefly until thoroughly heated through, then remove the wok from the heat. Make a deep cut into the potatoes and fluff up the flesh with a fork, spoon the filling into the potatoes and serve immediately.

TIME: *Preparation takes about 15 minutes.*
Marinate for at least 1 hour.
Cooking takes approximately 5 minutes.

23

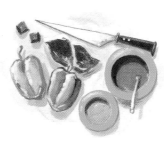

Italian Ham & Cheese

SERVES 4

A *quick and easy filling with a decidedly European feel*

INGREDIENTS
4 large baking potatoes
4 ounces fresh Parmesan cheese
¼ cup butter
4 slices Parma ham, cut into thin strips
2 teaspoons horseradish sauce
½ cup fresh sour cream

Begin by setting the potatoes to bake in a hot oven as recommended in the introduction.

Using a potato peeler, thinly slice the Parmesan cheese into wafer-thin slivers.

When the potatoes are cooked, cut in half and scoop out the flesh. Mash well with the butter.

Reserve a little of the cheese, and beat the remainder into the potato along with the ham and horseradish sauce.

Pile the potato mixture back into the potato skins and return to the oven for 10 minutes to heat through.

Place on a serving dish and top with the sour cream and reserved cheese. Serve immediately.

TIME: *Preparation takes about 5 minutes. Reheating takes approximately 10 minutes.*
MICROWAVE NOTES: *If cooking the potatoes in a microwave, reheat for 1 minute.*

25

Crunchy Chicken

SERVES 4

This dish is great for using up leftover chicken

INGREDIENTS
4 large baking potatoes
1 pound cooked chicken, cut into bite-size pieces
4 small stalks celery, thinly sliced or chopped
4 ounces corn, defrosted if frozen
½ cup Greek yogurt
salt and pepper
2 tablespoons chopped fresh mint
few drops of Tabasco sauce
fresh mint leaves for garnish

▌Begin by setting the potatoes to bake in a hot oven as recommended in the introduction.
▌Put the chicken, celery and corn in a bowl.
▌Mix together the yogurt, seasoning, chopped mint and Tabasco, and pour over the chicken mixture, stirring until well coated.
▌When the potatoes are cooked, cut in half and mash the flesh slightly. Spoon the chicken mixture on top, garnish with fresh mint and serve immediately.

TIME: *Preparation takes about 5 minutes.*
VARIATION: *Use ham if you do not have any leftover chicken. Cooked turkey can also be used, making this an ideal Christmas-time lunch.*

Cheese & Bacon

SERVES 4

An ideal midweek supper dish

INGREDIENTS
4 large baking potatoes
8 ounces bacon, diced
2 small onions, finely chopped
5 tablespoons sunflower oil
salt and pepper
4 ounces Gruyère cheese, grated
4 tablespoons fresh breadcrumbs

▌Begin by setting the potatoes to bake in a hot oven as recommended in the introduction.
▌Mix together the bacon and onion.
▌Heat the oil in a frying pan and fry the bacon and onion gently for 5 minutes.
▌Drain off any liquid, then increase the heat and cook for about 5 minutes or until beginning to crisp.
▌Cut the cooked potato in half and scoop out the flesh into a bowl. Mash well.
▌Beat the bacon and onion into the potato and season to taste with salt and pepper. Mix in half the cheese, then pile back into the potato skins.
▌Mix the remaining cheese with the breadcrumbs and sprinkle over the potatoes. Place under a preheated broiler until golden.

TIME: *Preparation takes about 10 minutes.*
COOKING *takes approximately 15 minutes.*

Mini Saté & Peanut Sauce

SERVES 4

The potatoes are topped with beef kebabs and an aromatic sauce

INGREDIENTS

4 large baking potatoes

8 ounces fillet or sirloin steak, cut into small cubes

Grated zest and juice of ½ lime

3 tablespoons sunflower oil

½ teaspoon crushed dried chilies

pinch of turmeric

pinch of cumin

1 small onion, chopped

¼ teaspoon chili powder

6 tablespoons peanut butter

salt and pepper

fresh cilantro, to garnish

▌ Begin by setting the potatoes to bake in a hot oven as recommended in the introduction.

▌ Thread the steak onto 8 cocktail sticks. Place in a shallow dish. Mix together the lime zest, juice, 2 tablespoons of the oil, chilies, turmeric and cumin. Pour over the meat.

▌ Allow the meat to marinate for 30 minutes, turning occasionally.

▌ Heat the remaining oil in a small saucepan and fry the onion until soft.

▌ Add the chili powder and fry for 1 minute, then stir in 6 tablespoons water and the peanut butter. Simmer gently for 5 minutes, stirring occasionally.

▌ Cook the kebabs under a preheated broiler for 5–10 minutes, turning once.

▌ When the potatoes are cooked, cut the tops off each one and scoop the flesh into a bowl. Mash well. Season with salt and pepper and pile back into the potato skins. Spoon the peanut sauce on top and sprinkle with a little chopped fresh cilantro. Serve with the kebabs and garnish with a sprig of cilantro.

TIME: *Preparation takes about 10 minutes plus 30 minutes marinating. Cooking takes approximately 15 minutes.*

VARIATION: *Use skinned and boned chicken breasts in place of the steak.*

27

Fragrant Lamb in Rosemary Gravy

SERVES 4

Using fresh herbs in the marinade intensifies the wonderful flavors

INGREDIENTS

4 large baking potatoes

2 cloves garlic

salt and pepper

2 tablespoons olive oil

4 tablespoons dry white wine

juice and zest of ½ lemon

2 tablespoons chopped fresh rosemary

12 ounces fresh lamb fillet

1 teaspoon cornstarch

butter

Begin by setting the potatoes to bake in a hot oven as recommended in the introduction.

Peel and roughly chop the garlic, sprinkle with a little salt and crush to a smooth paste with the handle of a knife. Mix the garlic paste with the olive oil, white wine and the juice and zest of the lemon.

Bruise the rosemary with the handle of a knife and add to the marinade.

Slice the lamb into ¼-inch slices and pour over the marinade, leave for an hour for the flavors to infuse.

When the potatoes are nearly cooked, remove the lamb from the marinade and arrange it on a baking sheet, season generously with salt and fresh black pepper.

Place under a preheated broiler and cook until there is just a slight pinkness left in the center of the lamb, turning once during cooking.

While the lamb is broiling, heat the marinade in a saucepan and thicken with a little cornstarch made into a paste with cold water, season with salt and pepper and keep hot.

Cut a deep cross into the baked potatoes and squeeze gently from the base of the potato to expose the flesh, than melt a little butter in each one. Share the cooked lamb among the potatoes and pour over the thickened gravy, garnish with a sprig of fresh rosemary and serve immediately.

TIME: *Preparation takes about 10 minutes.*
Marinate for at least 1 hour.
Cooking takes approximately 15 minutes.

Barbecued Belly of Pork

SERVES 4

The barbecue sauce really brings out the flavors of the meat

INGREDIENTS
4 large baking potatoes
1 pound lean belly of pork
butter

FOR THE BARBECUE SAUCE:
1 tablespoon clear honey
2 tablespoons thin-cut marmalade
2 tablespoons soya sauce
1 tablespoon white wine vinegar
1 teaspoon paprika
1 clove garlic, crushed
tomato ketchup to taste

Cut away any little pieces of bone remaining on the belly of pork and remove the skin – this is best achieved using a pair of kitchen scissors.

Cut each length of pork crosswise into roughly 1½-inch lengths and place in a bowl.

Mix all the barbecue sauce ingredients together and pour over the prepared pork, stir together well and allow to stand long enough for the flavors to infuse.

Set the potatoes to bake as recommended in the introduction.

When the potatoes are three-quarters cooked, remove the pork from the barbecue sauce and arrange on a tinfoil-covered baking sheet.

Place under a preheated broiler and cook for approximately 15 minutes, turning regularly and brushing with any remaining barbecue sauce, until the meat is nicely browned and crispy.

Cut a deep cross into each baked potato and melt a little butter into the flesh, share the barbecued pork evenly among the potatoes and serve immediately.

TIME: *Preparation takes about 15 minutes.*
Marinate for at least 30 minutes.
Cooking takes approximately 15 minutes.

31

Chicken & Apricot Curry

SERVES 4

*Spicy curries go as well with potatoes as they do with their
traditional accompaniment — rice*

INGREDIENTS

4 large baking potatoes

½ teaspoon chili powder

2 teaspoons garam masala

1 inch piece root ginger, peeled and grated

salt

2 cloves garlic, crushed

4 chicken breasts, skinned, boned
and cut into bite-size pieces

2 tablespoons ghee or sunflower oil

1 tablespoon curry paste

1 large onion, cut into wedges

14-ounce can chopped tomatoes

2 ounces no-soak dried apricots, chopped

1 teaspoon sugar

4 tablespoons white wine vinegar

❙ Begin by setting the potatoes to bake in a hot
oven as recommended in the introduction.

❙ Mix together the chili powder, garam masala,
ginger, salt and garlic. Spread this over the
chicken, and toss to coat well.

❙ Allow the chicken to marinate for 1–2 hours to
absorb the flavors.

❙ Melt the ghee or heat the oil in a large frying pan
and add the spiced chicken and the curry paste.

❙ Toss over a high heat for 5 minutes until the
chicken is browned.

❙ Remove from the pan and set aside.

❙ Add the onion along with a little more ghee
or oil if necessary, and fry for 5 minutes until
just soft.

❙ Return the chicken to the pan and add the
tomatoes and apricots. Cook for 20 minutes.

❙ Stir in the sugar and vinegar, and cook for a
further 10 minutes.

❙ Split the potatoes in half and top with the curry.

TIME: *Preparation takes about 15 minutes plus
2 hours marinating.*

Cooking takes approximately 40 minutes.

VARIATION: *Diced turkey can be used in this recipe
in place of the chicken.*

SERVING IDEA: *This dish is delicious served with a
tomato and onion salad.*

32

Fava Beans & Bacon

SERVES 4

Fava beans and bacon make a delicious combination

INGREDIENTS

4 large baking potatoes

2 tablespoons sunflower oil

1 onion, chopped

1 clove garlic, crushed

4 ounces diced bacon (smoked if possible)

6 ounces frozen fava beans

salt and pepper

1 tablespoon chopped fresh mixed herbs

or 1 teaspoon dried mixed herbs

½ cup grated Cheddar cheese

2 tablespoons grated Parmesan cheese

fresh herbs to garnish

Begin by setting the potatoes to bake in a hot oven as recommended in the introduction.

Heat the oil in a frying pan and fry the onion for 3–4 minutes or until beginning to soften.

Add the garlic and fry gently for 1 minute.

Increase the heat and add the bacon, then fry for about 5 minutes or until beginning to crisp.

Cook the beans in boiling water for 3–4 minutes, drain well and add to the pan. Stir in the salt, pepper and herbs.

When the potatoes are cooked, cut in half and scoop out the flesh. Mash well.

Mix the beans and bacon into the potato and pile back into the potato skins.

Mix together the two cheeses and sprinkle over the potatoes. Brown under a preheated broiler and serve immediately. Garnish with mixed herbs.

TIME: *Preparation takes about 10 minutes. Cooking takes approximately 15 minutes.*

SERVING IDEA: *Serve as a light meal or as an accompaniment to other dishes.*

Calves Liver with Sweet Red Onions

SERVES 4

A *delightful mix of savory and sweet flavors*

INGREDIENTS
4 large baking potatoes
1½ pounds calves liver
2 egg yolks, lightly beaten
brown breadcrumbs for coating
salt and black pepper
olive oil
1 pound red onions, peeled and finely sliced
1 tablespoon brown sugar

Set the potatoes to bake in a hot oven as recommended in the introduction.

When the potatoes are three-quarters cooked, begin preparing the topping.

Rinse the liver under cold running water and pat dry with paper towel, then slice into strips of roughly equal sizes.

Place the egg yolks and breadcrumbs with a little seasoning in separate bowls. Dip each piece of liver in the egg yolk and then coat thoroughly with the seasoned crumbs. Arrange the prepared liver on a lightly oiled baking sheet and put to one side.

Heat ½ tablespoon of olive oil and gently fry the onions until soft and slightly browned, stir in the brown sugar and remove from the heat.

Place the crumbed liver under a preheated broiler for approximately 6 minutes, carefully turning once during cooking. The cooked liver should remain pink on the inside but crisp and golden on the outside.

Cut a deep cross in the top of each baked potato and gently squeeze from the base so the fluffy potato flesh is exposed.

Spoon the onion and cooking juices followed by the crisp liver over the top of each potato, finish with a twist of freshly ground pepper and serve.

TIME: *Preparation takes about 15 minutes. Cooking takes approximately 10 minutes.*

34

Smoked Haddock & Tomato

SERVES 4

Smoked fish gives a lovely flavor to potatoes

INGREDIENTS
4 large baking potatoes
8 ounces smoked haddock, skinned
4 tablespoons milk
knob of butter
salt and pepper
pinch of grated nutmeg
1 beef tomato, chopped
1 teaspoon chopped fresh parsley
fresh parsley to garnish

Begin by setting the potatoes to bake in a hot oven as recommended in the introduction.
Put the haddock in an ovenproof dish. Pour over the milk and add the butter. Season with salt and pepper. Cover with tinfoil.
About 20 minutes before the end of the potatoes' cooking time, place the fish on a lower shelf in the oven. Cook until it flakes easily with a fork.

Cut a lid off the cooked potatoes and discard. Scoop out the flesh and place in a large bowl. Carefully add the liquid from the fish and the nutmeg. Season to taste and mash well.
Beat the tomato pieces into the potato along with the chopped parsley.
Pile the potato flesh back into the skins.
Pile the flaked fish on top of the potato and serve garnished with fresh parsley.

TIME: *Preparation takes about 10 minutes. Cooking takes approximately 20 minutes.*
VARIATION: *Use another smoked fish in this recipe, such as smoked mackerel, cod or herring.*
COOK'S TIP: *Cooking the fish in the oven at the same time as the potatoes is a good way of saving fuel.*
MICROWAVE NOTES: *This recipe is not suitable for cooking in a microwave.*

36

$\mathscr{S}$hrimp & $\mathscr{A}$vocado

SERVES *4*

You can use smaller potatoes and serve this dish as a starter

INGREDIENTS

4 large baking potatoes

1 ripe avocado, peeled and cubed

grated zest and juice of ½ lime

4 ounces cooked and shelled shrimp

1 tomato, skinned and chopped

4 tablespoons Greek yogurt

1 tablespoon tomato paste

dash of Tabasco

salt and pepper

ground paprika

 Begin by setting the potatoes to bake in a hot oven as recommended in the introduction.

 Toss the avocado pieces in the lime juice to prevent discoloration.

 Add the shrimp and tomato and stir to combine.

 In a small mixing bowl, mix together the yogurt, tomato paste, Tabasco, seasoning and lime zest.

 Pour over the shrimp and toss until well coated.

 When the potatoes are cooked, cut a cross in the top of each one. Gently squeeze each potato to open out the cross slightly.

 Pile the shrimp on top and garnish with a sprinkling of paprika.

TIME: *Preparation takes about 15 minutes.*
WATCHPOINT: *Avocados are ripe when they yield slightly upon being gently squeezed. If very soft, they will be mushy and will not have a good flavor.*

Scrambled Eggs & Smoked Salmon

SERVES 4

An ideal special supper or brunch dish

INGREDIENTS
4 large baking potatoes
4 eggs
¼ cup milk
salt and pepper
pinch of grated nutmeg
pinch of cayenne pepper
¾ cup butter
8 ounces smoked salmon, cut into strips
1 bunch chives, snipped
broiled tomatoes and fresh chives to serve

▌ Set the potatoes to bake in a hot oven.
▌ Put the eggs in a small bowl with the milk, seasoning, nutmeg and cayenne and beat with a fork until frothy.
▌ When the potatoes are cooked, cut in half and dot with butter. Mash the flesh and keep warm.
▌ Melt the remaining butter in a small saucepan and pour in the egg mixture. Cook over a low heat, stirring constantly, to scramble the egg as it cooks.
▌ When almost set, stir in the smoked salmon and chives and cook for a few seconds. Pile onto the potatoes and serve with broiled tomatoes and garnish with fresh chives.

TIME: *Preparation takes about 5 minutes.*
Cooking takes approximately 5 minutes.

Piquant Flaked Salmon

SERVES 4

The perfect healthy lunchtime snack

INGREDIENTS
4 large baking potatoes
14-ounce can red salmon, drained
5 tablespoons white wine vinegar
juice of ½ lime
black pepper
roughly chopped cilantro to garnish

▌ Begin by setting the potatoes to bake in a hot oven as recommended in the introduction.
▌ Carefully remove the salmon from the can and place it in a bowl. Using a fork break it into its natural flakes.
▌ Put the wine vinegar, lime juice and black pepper into a screw-top jar and shake well to mix it together. Pour the mixture over the salmon and allow it to soak into the fish while the potatoes finish baking.
▌ When the potatoes are cooked, split them down the center and share the salmon among them, garnish each potato with plenty of chopped cilantro and serve.

TIME: *Preparation takes about 5 minutes.*

Fresh Steamed Mussels with Parsley

SERVES 4

A *great lunchtime dish, so evocative of rustic French cafés*

INGREDIENTS

2 pints small fresh mussels

4 large baking potatoes

¼ cup butter

1 large onion, finely chopped

⅔ cup white wine

6 tablespoons sour cream

fresh parsley, chopped

If time allows, it is a good idea to feed the mussels for 24 hours prior to cooking because this removes any impurities that may be inside the shell. To do this, scrub the shells thoroughly, place the mussels in a bowl of fresh cold water and sprinkle a small amount of flour over the surface of the water.

Set the potatoes to bake in a hot oven as recommended in the introduction.

When the potatoes are nearly cooked, melt the butter in a large saucepan with a tight-fitting lid and fry the onion until soft but not colored.

Drain the water from the mussels and rinse well. Discard any that have already opened.

Add the mussels to the saucepan along with the white wine and cover with the lid, increase the heat and allow a few minutes for the mussels to steam.

When the majority of shells have opened and the mussels inside are a wonderful pink/orange color remove the pan from the heat.

Split the baked potatoes down the center and, using a slotted spoon, divide the cooked mussels among the four potatoes. Any shells that remain closed should be discarded.

Quickly reheat the cooking liquor and stir in the sour cream, gently warm it through before pouring a little over each potato.

Finish with a generous handful of chopped parsley and serve with crusty French bread.

TIME: *Allow 24 hours for the mussels to clean. Cooking takes approximately 5–10 minutes.*

41

Smoked Herring & Eggs

SERVES 4

This first-rate fish dish is ideal for brunch

INGREDIENTS
4 large baking potatoes
2 pairs fresh smoked herring
butter
2 hard-boiled eggs, roughly chopped
3 ounces frozen peas, defrosted
salt and pepper
¼ cup grated red Leicester cheese
¼ cup grated Cheddar cheese
Hard-boiled egg slices and sprigs of dill, to garnish

Begin by setting the potatoes to bake in a hot oven as recommended in the introduction.

Dot the fish with butter and wrap them in tinfoil, place in a preheated oven, 350°F, for 20 minutes.

Put the chopped egg in a mixing bowl with the peas. When the fish is cooked pour the juices over the egg and peas.

Carefully remove all the flesh from the herring, flake it into pieces and add it to the bowl.

When the potatoes are cooked, cut in half and scoop out the flesh. Mash well and add to the fish.

Beat the fish and potato together until well combined. Taste and season as desired.

Pile back into the potato skins. Mix together the two cheeses and sprinkle on top. Return to the oven for 10–15 minutes to heat through and brown the cheese.

Serve garnished with egg slices and sprigs of dill.

TIME: *Preparation takes about 5 minutes. Cooking takes approximately 30 minutes.*
MICROWAVE NOTES: *If cooking the potatoes in a microwave, reheat for 1½ minutes on 100% (high).*

42

*S*hrimp in *L*ime & *D*ill *M*ayonnaise

SERVES 4

This fresh-tasting mayonnaise tastes great with fish

INGREDIENTS

4 large baking potatoes

4 tablespoons chopped fresh dill

6 tablespoons olive oil

juice of ½ lemon

salt and pepper

20 large cooked shrimp, shelled

juice and zest of 1 lime

1¼ cups fresh mayonnaise

12 cherry tomatoes, halved

dill sprigs and lime segments to garnish

▌ Begin by setting the potatoes to bake in a hot oven as recommended in the introduction.

▌ Mix together 2 tablespoons of the chopped dill, olive oil, lemon juice and seasoning and pour over the shrimp. Put to one side while the flavors infuse.

▌ Add the juice and zest of the lime and the remaining chopped dill to the mayonnaise, season with some black pepper and beat together thoroughly. Chill in the refrigerator until required.

▌ When the potatoes are cooked drain the marinade from the shrimp and combine them with the tomato halves and the mayonnaise.

▌ Cut the potatoes almost in half and lightly break up the flesh with a fork. Spoon the filling carefully over each potato.

▌ Garnish with sprigs of dill and serve with segments of lime and a twist of fresh pepper.

TIME: *Preparation takes about 10 minutes. Marinate for at least 45 minutes.*

43

Tuna with Multi-colored Peppers

SERVES 4

The ginger in this recipe gives it a slightly exotic flavor

INGREDIENTS

4 large baking potatoes

2 tablespoons olive oil

½ green bell pepper, seeded and diced

½ red bell pepper, seeded and diced

½ yellow bell pepper, seeded and diced

½ teaspoon black or white pepper

1 inch piece root ginger, peeled and grated

½ teaspoon crushed dried chilies

salt and pepper

7-ounce can tuna chunks, drained

grated zest of ½ lemon

1 tablespoon lemon juice

½ cup grated Cheddar cheese

▌Begin by setting the potatoes to bake in a hot oven as recommended in the introduction.

▌Heat the oil in a frying pan and toss the peppers in the oil. Cook over a moderate heat for 5 minutes, stirring regularly until soft and beginning to brown slightly.

▌Add the ginger and crushed chilies, and season with salt and pepper.

▌Add the tuna, lemon zest and juice to the pan. Cook over a low heat for 2–3 minutes or until the tuna is hot.

▌When the potatoes are cooked, cut in half and scoop the flesh into a bowl. Mash well.

▌Add the tuna mixture to the potato and then mix well.

▌Pile back into the potato skins and sprinkle with grated cheese. Return to the oven for 10 minutes or until the cheese melts.

TIME: *Preparation takes about 10 minutes. Cooking takes approximately 15 minutes plus reheating.*

VARIATION: *Use canned salmon in place of the tuna.*

MICROWAVE NOTES: *If cooking the potatoes in a microwave, reheat for 2–3 minutes on 100% (high).*

45

Rolled Fresh Anchovies

SERVES 4

Full of the tastes of the Mediterranean

INGREDIENTS
4 large baking potatoes
16 fresh anchovies, filleted
6 fresh red chilies, seeded and finely sliced
1¼ cups virgin olive oil
16 pitted black olives
unsalted butter

Begin by setting the potatoes to bake in a hot oven as recommended in the introduction.

Add chili slices to the olive oil. For a really good chili oil it is best to leave the chilies marinating for at least 10 days; however, this is not essential and the oil can in fact be used quite soon after being prepared.

Roll each anchovy around an olive and spike them through with a cocktail stick. Place on a dish and pour over the chili oil. Leave to marinate.

When the potatoes are cooked, cut a deep cross into each one and gently push from the base of the potato to expose the flesh. Place a knob of butter on each potato and lay 4 of the marinated anchovies on top, pour over 1 teaspoon of the flavored marinade and serve at once.

TIME: *Preparation takes about 10 minutes. Marinate for at least 30 minutes.*

COOK'S TIP: *Do not be discouraged from using anchovies in this way as their flavor is much more subtle than that of the tinned variety.*

Sardine & Tomato Hash

SERVES 4

A simple standby meal

INGREDIENTS
4 large baking potatoes
2 tablespoons olive oil
1 bunch scallions, sliced
4 cloves garlic, crushed
4 stalks celery, chopped
few fresh basil leaves
2 x 14 ounce cans sardines in tomato sauce
salt and pepper
knob of butter
dash of Worcestershire sauce

Begin by setting the potatoes to bake in a hot oven as recommended in the introduction.

Heat the oil in a small pan and fry the scallions and garlic for 2–3 minutes or until the scallions are soft.

Add the celery and cook for another 3–4 minutes.

Tear the basil into small pieces and add along with the sardines in their sauce. Mix well. Season and add the butter and Worcestershire sauce.

When the potatoes are cooked, scoop out the flesh, keeping it as whole as possible, and cut into cubes.

Add to the pan and toss over the heat for a few minutes before piling back into the potato skins. Serve immediately.

TIME: *Preparation takes about 10 minutes. Cooking takes approximately 20 minutes.*

Seafood & Tomato

SERVES *4*

P*repared, mixed seafood is readily available*

INGREDIENTS
4 large baking potatoes
2 tablespoons sunflower oil
1 clove garlic, crushed
12 ounces tomatoes, skinned and chopped
5 tablespoons white wine
1 pound mixed seafood, e.g. squid,
mussels, shrimp
2 tablespoons chopped fresh parsley

Begin by setting the potatoes to bake in a hot oven as recommended in the introduction.
Heat the oil in a saucepan and fry the garlic.
Add the tomatoes and sauté for 2 minutes, then stir in the wine and bring to a boil.
Reduce the heat and simmer for 30 minutes or until thickened slightly.
Stir in the seafood and simmer gently for 10 minutes or until piping hot. Stir in the parsley.
If the sauce is still runny, thicken with a little cornstarch, mixed to a paste with cold water.
When the potatoes are cooked, cut in half and mash the flesh slightly if you wish. Spoon the seafood mixture on top and serve immediately.

TIME: *Preparation takes about 10 minutes.*
Cooking takes approximately 45 minutes.

Tangy Crab & Shrimp

SERVES *4*

A *light and attractive seafood dish*

INGREDIENTS
4 large baking potatoes
10-ounce can crab-meat, drained
4 ounces cooked and shelled shrimp
1 bunch scallions, sliced
1 cup mayonnaise
grated zest and juice of 1 lime
salt and pepper

Begin by setting the potatoes to bake in a hot oven as recommended in the introduction.
Put the crab-meat in a bowl and stir in the shrimp and sliced scallions.
Mix together the mayonnaise, lime zest and juice. Pour over the fish and stir until well combined. Season to taste with salt and pepper.
When the potatoes are cooked, cut in half, scoop out the flesh and mash well.
Pile back into the potato skins and top with the crab mixture.

TIME: *Preparation takes about 5 minutes.*
VARIATION: *Use crab sticks if preferred.*

Squid in Spinach & Cream Sauce

SERVES 4

A *great-tasting fish in a delicious, colorful sauce*

INGREDIENTS
4 large baking potatoes
1 pound small fresh squid, cleaned (with
quills removed)
4 tablespoons olive oil
1 onion, finely chopped
2 cloves garlic
3 ounces frozen spinach, defrosted
1¼ cups heavy cream
salt and pepper
fresh chopped parsley

Begin by setting the potatoes to bake in a hot oven as recommended in the introduction.

Wash the squid under cold running water and pat dry with paper towel, cut into ¼-inch rings and set to one side.

When the potatoes are nearly cooked heat 2 tablespoons of the olive oil in a frying pan and fry the chopped onion until soft but not colored. Skin and crush the garlic and add to the pan, frying for a further minute.

Squeeze as much liquid from the spinach as possible before adding it to the pan and heating through. Stir in the cream, season well with salt and fresh black pepper and throw in a handful of chopped parsley. Allow to simmer for a further minute or two, stirring to combine all the flavors, then reduce the heat to a very low simmer.

Heat the remainder of the olive oil in a separate pan and add the squid rings, cook until the liquid has run from the fish. This will take only a couple of minutes.

Drain the liquid from the squid and stir the fish into the cream sauce, increase the heat and allow the sauce to simmer gently for a further 5 minutes.

Split the baked potatoes through the middle and share the sauce among them, finish with a little more chopped parsley and serve immediately.

TIME: *Preparation takes about 5 minutes. Cooking takes approximately 15 minutes.*

Deep-fried Deviled Whitebait

SERVES 4

Crispy whitebait makes an unusual potato filling

INGREDIENTS
4 large baking potatoes
1 pound whitebait
½ cup milk
oil for frying
2 lemons

FOR THE COATING
1 tablespoon flour
1 teaspoon English mustard powder
1 teaspoon cayenne pepper
pinch of ground ginger
salt and pepper

Begin by setting the potatoes to bake in a hot oven as recommended in the introduction.

When the potatoes are nearly cooked, rinse the whitebait under cold water and drop them into the milk.

Mix together the ingredients for the coating and pass it through a sieve to remove any lumps. Drain any excess milk from the fish and mix them into the coating.

Heat the oil for deep frying. A simple test to check that the oil is hot enough is to drop a small cube of bread into the pan – if it browns within 30 seconds the oil has reached the correct temperature.

Shake the whitebait in a sieve to remove any excess coating and fry the fish in several batches to prevent them from sticking together. Keep the cooked fish warm in the oven while frying the remainder.

Cut a deep cross into each potato and gently ease it open, loosen the flesh with a fork and melt a generous portion of butter over it.

Share the whitebait among the potatoes and finish the dish with a little fresh black pepper and wedge of lemon before serving.

TIME: *Preparation takes about 10 minutes.*
Cooking takes approximately 10 minutes.

52

Mixed Bean Salad

SERVES 4

The beans turn simple baked potatoes into a wholesome and filling meal

INGREDIENTS

4 large baking potatoes

8-ounce can red kidney beans, drained and rinsed

8-ounce can lima beans, drained and rinsed

16-ounce can aduki beans, drained and rinsed

7-ounce can cut green beans, drained and rinsed

2 ounces corn, defrosted

2 stalks celery, sliced

1 clove garlic

½ teaspoon salt

1 teaspoon mustard powder

1 tablespoon cider vinegar

freshly ground black pepper

6 tablespoons olive oil

1 teaspoon snipped fresh chives

1 teaspoon chopped fresh tarragon

1 teaspoon chopped fresh parsley

knob of butter

Begin by setting the potatoes to bake in a hot oven as recommended in the introduction.

Put the beans in a bowl and toss to mix. Stir in the corn and celery.

Using a pestle and mortar, pound the garlic and salt to a paste. Add the mustard powder, vinegar and pepper and mix thoroughly. Gradually blend in the olive oil.

Transfer the garlic mixture to a small cup and then add the herbs, whisking with a fork until well blended.

Pour over the beans and toss until all the beans are well coated in the dressing.

When the potatoes are cooked, cut the tops off each one and scoop out the flesh.

Add a knob of butter and sprinkle with a little black pepper. Mash well. Pile back into the potato skins and serve with the bean salad.

TIME: *Preparation takes about 10 minutes.*

54

Welsh Tatties

SERVES 4

These potatoes are filled with leeks and a creamy cheese sauce

INGREDIENTS
4 large baking potatoes
¼ cup butter
1 pound leeks, thinly sliced
2 tablespoons all-purpose flour
1¼ cups milk
3 ounces Caerphilly cheese, crumbled
salt and pepper
cherry tomatoes to garnish

Begin by setting the potatoes to bake in a hot oven as recommended in the introduction.

Melt the butter in a saucepan and fry the leeks over a low heat for 6–10 minutes or until soft.

Stir in the flour and cook for 1 minute.

Remove from the heat and gradually add the milk, stirring well after each addition.

Return the pan to the heat and cook over a low heat until thickened, stirring constantly.

Add the cheese to the sauce and gently cook until most of the cheese melts.

When the potatoes are cooked, cut in half and scoop out the flesh. Mash well.

Add the leek mixture and beat until well combined. Season to taste. Spoon back into the potato skins and serve them garnished with cherry tomatoes.

TIME: *Preparation takes about 10 minutes. Cooking takes approximately 15 minutes.*

Spicy Vegetable Curry

SERVES 4

Curry served with baked potatoes makes a superb winter dish that is both warming and filling

INGREDIENTS

4 large baking potatoes

2 tablespoons ghee or sunflower oil

1 onion, chopped

2 cloves garlic, crushed

2 tablespoons ground cilantro

1 teaspoon ground cumin

½ teaspoon ground fenugreek

½ teaspoon ground turmeric

½ teaspoon chili powder

6 ounces small cauliflower flowerets

2 carrots, sliced

1 red bell pepper, seeded and
cut into small chunks

1 green bell pepper, seeded and
cut into small chunks

4 ounces mushrooms, halved or quartered

4 ounces green beans cut into short lengths

1¼ cups vegetable stock

1 teaspoon cornstarch (optional)

4 tablespoons natural yogurt

3 tablespoons crème fraîche

Begin by setting the potatoes to bake in a hot oven as recommended in the introduction.

Melt the ghee or heat the oil in a large saucepan and fry the onion for about 5 minutes or until soft.

Stir in the garlic and spices and cook over a low heat for 3 minutes, stirring constantly to prevent the spices from burning.

Add the vegetables and toss over the heat for 3–4 minutes.

Pour in the stock and bring to a boil. Reduce the heat, cover and simmer for 30 minutes, stirring occasionally, until the vegetables are tender.

Thicken the liquid with a little cornstarch mixed to a paste with cold water if you wish. Stir in the yogurt and crème fraîche and heat gently.

When the potatoes are cooked, cut in half and mash the flesh if liked. Spoon over the curry and serve immediately.

TIME: *Preparation takes about 15 minutes. Cooking time approximately 45 minutes.*

Spicy Guacamole Potatoes

SERVES 4

Add *a touch of spice to your potatoes with this Mexican dish*

INGREDIENTS

4 large baking potatoes

1 red or green chili

½ small onion, cut into chunks

1 clove garlic, crushed

2 tomatoes, skinned, seeded and roughly chopped

¼ teaspoon ground cumin

¼ teaspoon ground cilantro

1 large or 2 small ripe avocados

1 tablespoon chopped cilantro

1 tablespoon chopped parsley

2 teaspoons lemon juice

pinch of sugar

salt and pepper

tomato relish and fresh sour cream, to serve

Begin by setting the potatoes to bake in a hot oven as recommended in the introduction.

Cut the chili in half and remove the seeds if you wish. The seeds have the spicy heat of the chili and the end dish will be hotter if they are left in. Cut into chunks.

Put the onion, chili and garlic in a food processor and process briefly to chop roughly.

Add the chopped tomato to the mixture in the food processor along with the cumin and the ground cilantro.

Cut the avocado in half lengthwise. Twist the halves gently in opposite directions to separate. Remove the stone and scoop out the flesh, scraping the skin well.

Add the avocado to the mixture in the food processor with the chopped cilantro, parsley, lemon juice, sugar and seasoning. Process until the mixture is well combined with a fine, smooth consistency.

Chill until required.

When the potatoes are cooked, cut a cross in the top of each one. Gently squeeze each potato to open out the cross slightly.

Spoon the guacamole into the potatoes and top with tomato relish and sour cream.

TIME: *Preparation takes about 15 minutes.*

59

Curried Potato & Egg

SERVES 4

Hard-boiled eggs are tossed in a creamy, lightly spiced sauce,
then used to stuff the potato

INGREDIENTS
4 large baking potatoes
4 hard-boiled eggs, roughly chopped
3 stalks celery, sliced
2 scallions, sliced
1 small green bell pepper, seeded and chopped
1–2 teaspoons mild curry paste
2 tablespoons light cream
3 tablespoons mayonnaise
2 teaspoons mango chutney
paprika

Begin by setting the potatoes to bake in a hot oven as recommended in the introduction.

Put the chopped egg, celery, scallions and green bell pepper into a mixing bowl.

In a small bowl mix together the curry paste, cream, mayonnaise and chutney until they are well combined.

Pour over the chopped eggs and toss until well coated.

When the potatoes are cooked, cut a lid off each one and scoop out the flesh. Mash well.

Add the potato to the egg mixture and mix well. Pile back into the potato skins and return to the oven for 10 minutes to heat through. Sprinkle with paprika and serve immediately.

TIME: *Preparation takes about 10 minutes. Reheating takes approximately 10 minutes.*
MICROWAVE NOTES: *If cooking the potatoes in a microwave, reheat for 2–3 minutes on 100% (high).*

Ratatouille Topping

SERVES 4

Ratatouille is a Mediterranean dish that is ideal as a light meal
when served on potatoes

INGREDIENTS

4 large baking potatoes

2 tablespoons olive oil

1 Spanish onion, sliced

1 clove garlic, crushed

½ small eggplant, chopped

½ red bell pepper, seeded and chopped

½ green bell pepper; seeded and chopped

14-ounce can chopped tomatoes

1 tablespoon tomato paste

1 teaspoon chopped fresh oregano

few fresh basil leaves, torn into pieces

5 tablespoons red wine or vegetable stock

salt and pepper

▌Begin by setting the potatoes to bake in a hot oven as recommended in the introduction.

▌Heat the oil in a large frying pan and sauté the onion until beginning to soften. Add the garlic and cook for 1 minute.

▌Stir in the eggplant and peppers and fry over a medium heat until just beginning to soften.

▌Add the tomatoes, tomato paste, oregano, basil and wine or stock. Bring gently to a boil, then reduce the heat and simmer for 30 minutes or until the liquid has reduced slightly.

▌When the potatoes are cooked, cut in half and place on a serving plate.

▌Season the ratatouille to taste and spoon over the potatoes. Serve immediately.

TIME: *Preparation takes about 20 minutes.*
Cooking takes approximately 40 minutes.

61

Red Cabbage with Cashew Nuts

SERVES 4

An unusual and appetizing filling that can appeal to nonvegetarians too

INGREDIENTS
4 large baking potatoes
1 pound fresh red cabbage
1 onion
1 tablespoon brown sugar
⅓ cup cashew nuts
salt and pepper

Begin by setting the potatoes to bake in a hot oven as recommended in the introduction.

Remove the dark outer leaves from the cabbage and cut it in half through the stalk, then using a very sharp knife cut through the cabbage, across the leaves, to produce thin slices. Discard the stalk of the cabbage.

Peel and slice the onion, as thinly as possible, since it will have only the same amount of time to cook as the cabbage.

When the potatoes are three-quarters cooked, place the cabbage and onion slices and sufficient water to cover the base, in a saucepan with a tight-fitting lid.

Place over a high heat for 10–15 minutes until the cabbage has softened but still retains a certain crispness. At this point stir in the brown sugar and cashew nuts and allow to stand for a few minutes.

When the potatoes are cooked, remove from the oven and split them through the center. Season the filling with plenty of salt and freshly ground black pepper and pile spoonfuls into each potato.

TIME: *Preparation takes about 10 minutes. Cooking takes approximately 20 minutes.*

Spinach & Cream Cheese Soufflé

SERVES 4

These cheesy potatoes have a lighter texture than traditional baked potatoes

INGREDIENTS

4 large baking potatoes

2 tablespoons sunflower oil

1 small onion, finely chopped

6 ounces fresh spinach, washed

4 ounces cream cheese

salt and pepper

3 eggs, separated

1 tablespoon pine nuts

Begin by setting the potatoes to bake in a hot oven as recommended in the introduction.

Heat the oil in a saucepan and fry the onion until it has softened.

Add the spinach with just the water that clings to the leaves after washing and cook, covered, for about 5 minutes until wilted.

Drain off any water and roughly chop the spinach in a food processor.

Beat the spinach into the cream cheese. Season to taste.

When the potatoes are cooked, cut the tops off each one and scoop out the flesh. Mash well.

Beat the spinach mixture, egg yolks and pine nuts into the mashed potatoes.

Whisk the egg whites until standing in soft peaks, then carefully fold into the potato.

Spoon the mixture back into the potato skins.

Return to the oven and cook for 15–20 minutes or until risen and golden. Serve immediately.

TIME: *Preparation takes about 10 minutes. Cooking takes approximately 25 minutes.*

Crunchy Blue Cheese & Walnut

SERVES 4

*This is a lovely filling for summer baked potatoes since it has
a fresh flavor and crunchy texture*

INGREDIENTS

4 large baking potatoes
1 apple, sliced
lemon juice
4 stalks celery, sliced
¼ cup walnuts, chopped
5-ounce carton Greek yogurt
2 ounces blue cheese
salt and pepper
lemon twists, to garnish

Begin by setting the potatoes to bake in a hot oven as recommended in the introduction.

Toss the sliced apple in a little lemon juice to prevent discoloration.

Put the celery, apple and walnuts in a bowl and add the yogurt.

Crumble the blue cheese into the bowl, then toss all the ingredients together until well combined.

When the potatoes are cooked, cut a cross in the top of each one. Gently squeeze each potato to open out the cross slightly.

Season the potatoes with salt and pepper, then spoon the blue cheese mixture on top. Garnish with twists of lemon.

TIME: *Preparation takes about 10 minutes.*

65

Raisin Cauliflower Cheese

SERVES 4

A *great-tasting variation of a classic English dish*

INGREDIENTS
4 large baking potatoes
1 cauliflower
¼ cup butter
4 tablespoons flour
2⅓ cups milk
1 cup grated strong Cheddar cheese
salt and pepper
⅛ cup raisins

Begin by setting the potatoes to bake in a hot oven as recommended in the introduction.

Break off the outer leaves of the cauliflower and cut the heart into walnut-size flowerets. Rinse them thoroughly under cold running water.

Bring a saucepan of salted water to a boil and cook the cauliflower flowerets for 5–10 minutes until just tender. Drain off the water and spread them over paper towel to remove any excess moisture.

To make the sauce, gently melt the butter in a saucepan, add the flour and allow to cook together for a minute or two. Do not allow the mixture to color because this will affect the finished sauce.

Slowly add the milk a little at a time, stirring continuously until all the milk is incorporated and the sauce is smooth and thick. At this stage stir in two-thirds of the grated cheese and season generously with salt and freshly ground black pepper. Once the cheese has melted into the sauce remove the pan from the heat and put to one side.

Spread the blanched cauliflower over a lightly greased ovenproof dish and sprinkle with the raisins, pour over the cheese sauce and place in a preheated oven, 350°F, for 30 minutes.

Prior to serving, remove the cauliflower cheese from the oven, sprinkle with the remaining grated cheese and place under a hot broiler until a bubbling brown crust forms.

Split the baked potatoes and spoon in lots of cauliflower and cheese sauce, add a final twist of fresh black pepper and serve.

TIME: *Preparation takes about 10 minutes. Cooking takes approximately 45 minutes.*

Chick Pea Curry

SERVES 4

A *topping with a sophisticated taste*

INGREDIENTS
4 large baking potatoes
¼ cup butter
1 onion, finely chopped
2 teaspoons ground cilantro
½ teaspoon turmeric
½ teaspoon chili powder
2 x 14-ounce cans chick peas, drained
salt
⅔ cup plain full fat yogurt

▌Begin by setting the potatoes to bake in a hot oven as recommended in the introduction.

▌Melt the butter in a saucepan and gently fry the onion until golden brown. Add all the various spices to the pan and continue to cook briefly, then moisten with ¼ cup water and allow to heat through.

▌Add the drained chick peas and cover for a few minutes to allow the flavors to mix with the peas. Do not leave the pan for too long because the peas may begin to break up.

▌Remove the pan from the heat, season well with salt and gently stir in the yogurt.

▌Spoon the curry into the hot potato and serve with sweet mango chutney.

TIME: *Preparation takes about 5 minutes.*
Cooking takes approximately 20 minutes.

Coleslaw & Bavarian Cheese

SERVES 4

S *moked cheese added to tangy coleslaw*

INGREDIENTS
4 large baking potatoes
½ small head of white cabbage, thinly shredded
2 carrots, grated
½ green bell pepper, seeded and thinly sliced
3 ounces Bavarian smoked cheese
¼ cup mayonnaise
¼ cup fresh sour cream
salt and pepper
2 tablespoons cashew nuts, toasted

▌Begin by setting the potatoes to bake in a hot oven as recommended in the introduction.

▌Put the shredded cabbage in a large mixing bowl and add the grated carrot and sliced pepper. Add the cheese.

▌Mix together the mayonnaise and cream, and season well. Pour over the cabbage and toss until all the vegetables are coated.

▌When the potatoes are cooked, cut in half and mash the flesh if you wish. Serve with the coleslaw piled on top. Sprinkle with toasted cashew nuts.

TIME: *Preparation takes about 15 minutes.*

68

Broiled Goats' Cheese with Basil

SERVES 4

This recipe brings the flavors of Italy to mealtimes

INGREDIENTS

4 large baking potatoes
2 small goats' cheeses
virgin olive oil
salt and pepper
fresh basil leaves

Begin by setting the potatoes to bake in a hot oven as recommended in the introduction.

When the potatoes are nearly cooked, cut the cheeses into rounds and arrange them on a baking sheet. Brush each slice generously with some olive oil then turn them over, brush again and season them well with plenty of salt and freshly ground black pepper.

Place the prepared cheese under a preheated broiler and cook for a few minutes until the cheese is soft.

Slice the baked potatoes in half and gently fork over the inside to fluff it up a little, then carefully transfer the softened cheese slices onto the potato.

Finally, season once more with freshly ground black pepper and tear a few basil leaves and scatter over the potatoes before serving.

TIME: *Preparation takes about 5 minutes. Cooking takes approximately 5 minutes.*

SERVING IDEA: *This lunchtime snack has a very Mediterranean feel to it that's even more convincing served with a simple leaf salad and French dressing.*

69

Garlicky Mushroom & Hazelnuts

SERVES 4

Simple to prepare, this topping is quite irresistible

INGREDIENTS
4 large baking potatoes
6 tablespoons butter
1 small onion, peeled and finely chopped
3 cloves garlic, peeled and crushed
6 ounces small button mushrooms, quartered
3 tablespoons toasted hazelnuts, chopped
grated zest and juice of ½ lemon
salt and black pepper
2 tablespoons chopped parsley

Set the potatoes to bake in a hot oven as recommended in the introduction.

Melt the butter in a frying pan and fry the onion until just soft.

Stir in the garlic and cook for 1 minute.

Add the mushrooms to the pan and fry for 4–5 minutes until soft.

Stir in the hazelnuts, lemon zest, juice, seasoning and parsley. Cook gently for 2 minutes.

When the potatoes are cooked, cut a wedge out of each one, and mash the flesh if you wish. Spoon the mushroom and hazelnut mixture on top.

TIME: *Preparation takes about 10 minutes. Cooking takes approximately 10 minutes.*

Homemade Herb Mayonnaise

SERVES 4

The only way to experience really good mayonnaise is to make your own

INGREDIENTS
4 large baking potatoes
2 egg yolks
1 tablespoon lemon juice
1 teaspoon English mustard powder
¼ teaspoon salt
1¼ cups olive oil
¼ teaspoon freshly ground black pepper
1 tablespoon white wine vinegar
1 tablespoon each of chopped fresh parsley,
basil and oregano
sprigs of parsley to garnish

Begin by setting the potatoes to bake in a hot oven as recommended in the introduction.

To prepare the mayonnaise, place the egg yolks, lemon juice, mustard powder and salt in a bowl.

Beat thoroughly for a couple of minutes until all the ingredients are blended together.

Slowly add the olive oil a little at a time, beating well between each addition, until the sauce becomes thick and smooth. This process takes a little time; do not be tempted to rush by adding the oil too quickly because this may cause the mayonnaise to separate. If separation does occur, place a fresh egg yolk in a mixing bowl and gradually beat the mayonnaise into it, and this will correct the consistency.

To finish the mayonnaise stir in the pepper, wine vinegar and the fresh herbs and chill in the refrigerator.

When baked, split the potato across the middle and spoon in the mayonnaise, garnish with a sprig of parsley and serve immediately.

TIME: *Preparation takes about 20 minutes.*

Deep-fried Potato Skins with Salad

SERVES 4

This simple salad preparation mixes together strong flavors to good effect

INGREDIENTS
4 large baking potatoes
1 head of chicory
1 bunch of watercress
1 head of endive
good-quality oil for deep frying

FOR THE DRESSING:
2 tablespoons red wine vinegar
5 tablespoons olive oil
2 teaspoons Dijon mustard
salt and pepper

Begin by setting the potatoes to bake in a hot oven as recommended in the introduction. For this particular recipe it is a good idea to use the largest potatoes you can find.

Discard the outer leaves from the chicory and wash the remainder along with the watercress and endive in fresh cold water. Drain the leaves well and roughly tear the chicory and endive, place in a bowl along with the watercress.

To make the dressing place all the ingredients in a screw-top jar and shake vigorously for a few seconds, then pour over the salad and gently toss together.

When the potatoes are cooked cut them in half and scoop out the majority of the flesh, leaving an even thickness of potato all over.

Using sufficient oil to submerge the skins fully, heat to frying temperature and carefully, one at a time, fry each skin until it is crisp and brown. This will take approximately 2 minutes.

When cooked allow all the excess oil to run off the skins and leave to cool on paper towel.

Sprinkle the skins with a little salt and fill each one with salad, pouring over any dressing that has collected at the bottom of the bowl.

Serve immediately with lots of crusty French bread and chilled white wine.

TIME: *Preparation takes about 20 minutes. Cooking takes approximately 5 minutes.*

Carrot & Fava Bean Puffs

S E R V E S 4

F*orget the myths about soufflés, this one is easy to prepare*

INGREDIENTS

4 large baking potatoes

½ pound fresh carrots

¼ cup butter

4 tablespoons flour

1¼ cups milk

14-ounce can of fava beans, drained

¾ cup grated Parmesan cheese

4 eggs, separated

salt

cayenne pepper

Begin by setting the potatoes to bake in a hot oven as recommended in the introduction.

Peel the carrots and roughly chop, cook in plenty of boiling salted water until soft, then drain thoroughly and put to one side.

Melt the butter in a saucepan and add the flour, stir continuously for a couple of minutes, allowing the flour to cook but not color.

Slowly stir in the milk a little at a time until it has all been incorporated and you have a thick, smooth sauce, then remove the pan from the heat.

Place the cooked carrot, fava beans, grated cheese and egg yolks in a food processor and blend until smooth. Add this paste to the sauce and beat together well.

Season the mixture with a good pinch of salt and cayenne pepper, then pour the mixture into a mixing bowl.

When the potatoes are cooked cut them in half and using a spoon, remove the flesh from inside each one leaving a thin lining of potato in each skin. Mash the flesh of two of the potatoes and stir into the sauce. In a clean bowl whisk the egg whites until they form stiff peaks and carefully fold them into the sauce.

Arrange the skins on a baking sheet and fill each one two-thirds full with the soufflé mixture.

Place in a preheated oven, 375°F, for 20–25 minutes or until firm to the touch. Serve immediately.

TIME: *Preparation takes about 10 minutes. Cooking takes approximately 45 minutes.*

Index